The Optimist in Place

Kimberly Ann Priest

Harbor Editions
Small Harbor Publishing

Cover art by Laura Page
Cover design by Taylor Blevins
Book layout by Allison Blevins and Hannah Martin

THE OPTIMIST SHELTERS IN PLACE
KIMBERLY ANN PRIEST
ISBN 978-1-957248-01-1
Harbor Editions,
an imprint of Small Harbor Publishing

for the spider

ADVANCE PRAISE

Through the lens of collective tragedy and the lived experience of a woman alone, these neo-confessional poems balance the ache of imagining families "sobbing" in hospital parking lots with the personal loss of long isolation, the fresh finality of divorce, and even the tedious need to clean the shower.

—Lisa Fay Coutley, *tether*

The Optimist Shelters in Place is a deeply moving chapbook reminding us that COVID-19 is more than a pandemic of illness—it is a pandemic of loneliness, too. Rather than choosing despair, the speaker in these poems faces each day with empathy, humor, tenderness, and compassion. This remarkable book is necessary reading for anyone who wants to understand our historical moment—what it feels like to live in it and what it means to make the choice, day after day, to keep living through it.

—Jeffrey Bean, *Woman Putting on Pearls*

In her stellar and deeply relatable collection, Kimberly Ann Priest reveals the loneliness of a single American divorcee who is suddenly isolated in a pandemic-ravaged world. Full of grief and desperation, she recounts her coping strategies and acknowledges the underlying sorrow that many of our "joyful" social media posts attempt to mask. This collection also shows our constant need to conjure hope in the wake of tragedy.

—Meghan Sterling, *These Few Seeds*

CONTENTS

The Optimist Shelters in Place

THE OPTIMIST TAKES A PERSONALITY TEST

She leans into her plants. She speaks to them. She says,
soon it will be your season again.

The first breaths of spring ventilate through her apartment window,
filtered by its old screen mesh; it's the scent
of copper pennies
drowned in mossy puddles of freshly dropped rain.

The plants feel it too.

She tells them to think about new sills to adorn
in some inhabited future,
not to imagine this will be their final resting place. She tells them

what her daughter told her before leaving was deemed essential:
this is all temporal.

Lifting their stems like limbs she holds them toward
the extroverted world,
versatile and busy in her dreams and asks them
to dwell on impending playful sunlight or listen for the dead leaves
of last autumn fallen like voices of loved ones gone to seed.

Bury yourself, she says, in what funerals about us,
our faces masked winter-white;

feed the ghost like God's magic number, filling its mouth with sevens
until it greens up,
the ground repurposed, the tombstones lichen and bright.

THE OPTIMIST SPENDS A LOT OF TIME
ON PINTEREST

She folds and refolds the clothing in her closet
and her chest of drawers,
lovingly considering which items she will wear to her first
social outing, her first day at the beach, her first outdoor concert
and book store soirée,

as if her life has been anticipating *firsts* forever.

Like her daughter's first job disinfecting countertops, items, and walls
in a medical facility to kill contamination,
all anticipation because she was not employable until the virus came.

This, she thinks, is good: the job market, the market market
somehow stimulated in her daughter's favor. Funny
how things work out.

She sheds her excess time at home building a new wardrobe
from little digital tiles online under the heading *personal style,*
now and then clicking until she finds the item for sale
and spends her work-from-home pay on a few new pieces
to keep the economy going.

One does what one can to imagine a future as it has never been before.

THE OPTIMIST CANNOT FIND HER IPHONE

The day is full of mishaps.

First, she forgets to paint her toenails in case things change.
Then, the mailbox is not checked for a letter
she isn't expecting but hopes to get anyway. And after,

her alarm goes off and she cannot hit the tiny digital snooze
until she finds it sometime after 7 AM,
the time she intended to wake, not 4 AM,
the time she decided to wake; or rather,
the time decided for her when her fiancé [the one she does not have]
is caught smoking in her ex-husband's basement, and of course
this nightmare wakes her. Now,

she spends the afternoon avoiding CNN,
the last day of the third week in a row spent avoiding because
it will tell her nothing is beautiful.

Even the yogis are fearful, but pretending not to be by breathing a lot
into YouTube videos and teaching everyone else how to breathe.

She avoids them too. She knows how to breathe.

Yesterday, when the shower filled her bathroom with steam due to
no ventilation she gave up,
opened a window to the cold.

THE OPTIMIST HAS NO PLANS TO ALTER HER ROUTINE

She still spends an hour on the treadmill. Reads early morning.
Makes pour-over coffee and never finds anything to watch on TV.

This is the same life she had before the virus's intrusion.

Never a sniffle or cough.
Never a whole day in bed.

The covers are pulled tight over the pillows before breakfast as always,
the dishes washed, recycling stacked,
and she still makes time for a bit of personal prepping: lip gloss, messy
bun, a spritz of rosewater to brighten her face.

If today, she cannot manage a smile, she will post an old selfie
somewhere, just to be consistent.

On the windowsill, her plants curl over in response
to this grey April weekday
and she wonders how to help them stay cheered. For instance,
there are quotes she wants to share to social media platforms,
lifting the spirit of anyone despairing
such as: *mindset is everything, the best way out is always through,
the most reliable way to predict the future is to create it . . .*

but thinks better of this.

Instead, she draws a circle on a piece of notebook paper,
adds a smiling mouth and two eyes in its center,
then borders it with lines
of varied length—
tapes it to the window, waits for the foliage to unravel, look up.

THE OPTIMIST DEMANDS A SECOND CHANCE AT A VACATION

because Conde Nast has said we will have them again,
so she consoles her plants who were looking forward to the alone time
as much as she was looking forward to the not-alone time,
basking in some worthwhile experience, or just an experience
since experience itself is worthwhile.

She scrolls through each destination that offers a probable outcome
and enters another contest to win this travel package or that.

Her cousin has recently posted the death toll from somewhere
in New Jersey
and she decides she should have been a nurse so she could be
in New Jersey,
not here sheltered in place.

Looking out the window, she wonders what it means to be *essential*
after reading *There are no visitors allowed, so when someone passes,*
we are their family.

She wonders what it's like to have family standing in a parking lot
sheet white, shaken, mumbling, sobbing, staring at the brick hospital,
same color as the brick apartment building she views
outside her apartment window.

Not essential,
she scrolls through another possible vacation.

Not essential, no one will be waiting to hug her for her service
when this thing is over.

Not essential, no one has called her in weeks;
she'd rather die somewhere else than right here, alone.

THE OPTIMIST CONTINUES TO CONSIDER THE WEATHER

The word *report* has many definitions,
most of them formal, none of them conducive to the pajama pants
she's wearing as she fills out yet another computer-generated
questionnaire for work
while considering how lucky she is to be comfortable today;

the window open slightly exchanging old winter air for spring air,
a savory fifty-five degrees.

She warms her third cup of coffee in the microwave
while flipping through selections of tea: mint mandarin, vanilla
red chai, lotus flower Japanese green, lavender chamomile honey.

At 4 PM she will switch to wine.

The days are marked by frivolous choices.
She listens to the same podcasts between 6 and 8 PM, fluffs
the same pillows, writes the same lists
that she may or may not need; anything to feel a clock ticking,
the weather app still telling her when not to go outside
without a hooded sweatshirt.

She chooses one of the nine in her closet like someone gone shopping,
then walks the whole twelve blocks of the neighborhood around her
like someone exploring somewhere she has never been.

THE OPTIMIST TRIES A NEW RECIPE
FOR BBQ CHICKEN

She visits the grocery store for the fifth time since the executive orders
finding what she can. It seems
her local community survives on a steady diet of ground beef,
toilet paper, zinfandel, and corn.

Many of the aisles offer up slim pickings.

She's decided not to join the frenzy, make do. First
she searches for cucumbers,
discovering three lonely specimens badly battered and bruised
at the back of a produce shelf; buys zucchini instead.

Next, a young woman takes the last fresh baguette,
so she's forced to consider Danishes—but doesn't.

However, she splurges on good coffee since all the cheap stuff
has been hoarded.

In the canned goods aisle her options are okra, tomato paste,
and peaches; that's where she remembers a recipe for barbeque chicken
she hasn't made yet,
so she swoops up one of each
while at home a bag of frozen chicken waits in the freezer.

As do over three dozen tiny packets of honey,
the kind that come with warm biscuits at shabby local diners.
She hurries through the check out; she's been saving up for this!

THE OPTIMIST TAKES STOCK
OF HER PRIVILEGE

She has twenty-two cans of soup in the pantry. This will last her
twenty-two days,
so she writes a new shopping list.

Not because she needs anything now. Listing is her habit.

She has lists for what she wants in the house she will have in the future,
types of dogs she prefers for companions;
professional opportunities she hopes to take advantage of
should there ever be an opportunity;
locations she wants to travel to and the names of museums, cathedrals,
coffee shops, hiking trails, beaches, and breweries she plans
to visit if she ever gets there;
clothing items (kept in online carts) she wishes to buy someday;
the traits of men she's liked in the past simply to keep track
of what she might desire in a future partner if it ever comes to that;

the names of flowers too;

as well as all the things her family should have said to her
after the divorce (instead of what they said);
and the ways she'd like to be remembered by loved ones at her funeral.

Sometimes she lays out the dress, the shoes, the hair comb, and jewelry
she wants to wear into an afterlife:
a list in the shape of a body on the seldom used guest bed.

THE OPTIMIST DOESN'T WASH HER HAIR

To be honest, she thinks about death often.

Each time a leaf falls, a bell rings, the sky clouds over
but does not rain.

They call it *a plague,* and now she wishes someone had listened
when she told them her story,
most of it about conservation. For instance,
going nowhere, she decides to shower daily but not wash her hair
to save shampoo and avoid the damaging rigors of washing.

There are so many ways to be violent when trying not to be violent.

Last month, she reads, there were 4,000 suicides in this country
alone. These facts keep her mind busy.

At the University of Michigan, NODA was created to ensure
everyone died with someone at their bedside.
When her grandmother departed several years ago
a granddaughter was with her.

Just one.

A veteran in Portland, Maine, is working out his traumas
with poetry, she reads, *after* his wife has left him—a little boy
clinging to his arm in a photo puts her mind at ease.

How convenient her apartment when "out there" the dying;
how American avoidance—
realities we don't have to believe because they are unseen.

How lucky is a universe
not Biblical in its workings.

If a death angel passed by our doorposts looking for blood,
he'd find plenty:
on the bath towels, the kitchen towels, the bedsheets, the floor.

THE OPTIMIST LEAVES A DEAD SPIDER DEAD ON THE CARPET

There's still so much to do: laundry, emails, books to sort
and arrange.

The car hasn't been cleaned in months and then there's the shower,
dear God. She googles
"fun things to do in west Idaho." It's hard
not to get distracted; for instance, there's sun outside signaling
impulses she's forced to keep at bay.

It might be better if it rained for the next 30 days.

A siren whirs in the distance, a dog starts barking
hysterically, birds flutter inside a nearby tree and scurry skyward
like frightened banshee.

From underneath her coffee table a lone spider
plans a route of escape.

Quarantine is difficult for all sorts of creatures.

At dusk, when shadows brush the carpet a semi-cloudy grey,
he leaps out from under swimming over its follicles,
but not fast enough.
His smushed dot remains on the carpet for over three days.

This feels like a feeling even though it isn't,
and this feeling seems innocent enough.

THE OPTIMIST WANTS TO ASK A QUESTION

Scrolling through her Facebook feed is like walking through
a mine field of "doctor this" and "politician that."

She stifles a desire to know all the answers because *everyone*
has come to a conclusion
and, if nothing else, history has certainly divulged the dangers
of rightness—deadly.

Hence, it seems, our present moment.

Hence the photos she posts of the state park she visited on Sunday—
spacious landscape of dune sand and pine. There
she roamed the unbeaten path, burrowed the earth, and listened
to the rhythm of a lake that has known its own invasion—microbes
feasting on healthy bacteria living off its energy, taking it away.

Sometimes man gutting and wasting.

She finds a plastic bottle rested against a dried piece of wood
and resists the inclination to touch it, turns
her body back to the heartbeat of water. Buries her hand in beach
sand.

THE OPTIMIST BUYS AN EXPENSIVE BOTTLE OF WINE

Most days, she prefers a glass of blush; she loves an afternoon siesta.

Nothing has changed much now except that
it feels beautiful to hold a delicate glass vessel in her hand.

Yesterday, at the grocery store, she opted for a vintage
a bit pricier because the label was pretty, a farmhouse inked into
a fruitful backdrop, gold-gilded and muted
in time. She pours
the deep purple liquid into her slim ally, turns on
the radio, leans back, the juice smooth in her throat, sweet but subtle.

Someone is dying this way today,
head against a pillow, eyes drawn shut—siesta.

She didn't even need to buy the new bottle; her wine rack is full.

But she read on the internet
that the virus is killing even the young,
so she went shopping, groped red peppers in the produce section
long enough to see if he was still there working—the grocer
in his late-twenties—before choosing one.

He was.

As usual, he looked up when he sensed her, lingering briefly. Someday,
when the virus is over, she'll ask him for his number and a name.

THE OPTIMIST SCRAMBLES FOUR EGGS FOR BREAKFAST

then realizes this is too much but eats them anyway.

In North Carolina the death toll is 507.
But no one is talking much about North Carolina,
and she wonders what it's like to not be talked about much.

It's May now—
cherry trees outside her window in full bloom.
Someone will not outlive this second that she lifts her fork to face.
She imagines their loss of fresh eggs and coffee, the sound
of sizzling in a pan and Alanis Morrisette, the eucalyptus-candle-
mixed-with-burning-sage-incense scent.

This is a perfect sort of morning, a Saturday with no definite plans.

She lets the music forgive her for wanting to be transported
to sometime in the future when everyone has taught themselves
to necessarily forget. She hopes this won't be
a casualty for chickens—each egg dropped into a bucket, once again,
less sacred. Each morning's chance
to thank a gracious someone, sped through carelessly anew.

THE OPTIMIST REREADS MARY OLIVER'S DOG SONGS

The experts say another month indoors and maybe longer before
the worst of the virus is over. She's been expecting to hear of someone
she knows dying—but hasn't.

She listens for her plants to understand their conversations this tepid
Thursday afternoon when the sun is hidden from view.
Or is it Friday?
What ever happened to excitement for the weekend?

Cracking open a bottle of craft beer she's been saving
for a special occasion she decides *this* is a special occasion,
a *possibly-the-weekend-but-who-knows? party*.
She raises her beer to her favorite philodendron, embracing
the possible, declaring sarcastically *we're not dead yet!*

Each moment that slips by seems apocalyptic
but not apocalyptic,
the birds chirping tunes the way they always do in May.

It's a little rainy, but this is quite normal, and some buds are starting
to bloom on command.

In the apartment above her, a violinist practices as usual—
though perhaps a little longer. She pulls a book of poems off a shelf:
Percy is running, digging holes in the sand.

THE OPTIMIST CELEBRATES MOTHER'S DAY

First, a cup of coffee. Then, the birds. Now,
a single white rose perched in a vase.

Her daughter makes carrot cake and visits for two days.

She snuggles in her favorite chair, blanket-wrapped,
and listens to chatter outside and inside—her daughter full of speech.
Music. A note in a card to tell her of a mother's strength. So much
admiration.

For years, she's been waiting for magic;
for life to happen in some surprisingly beautiful way.

The frosting is homemade.

She heats a kettle of water for Moroccan mint tea, then sits beside
her daughter on a kitchen barstool.
The death toll is receding in her county this serene May day.

They sip and nibble together, talking about the future—together—
like sisters. Essential.

THE OPTIMIST USES BASIL & CUMIN

1.

She borrows the strange perch-*coo* of a dove
green-leaf shrouded and high, seeking a mate—and feels
this in her throat on a lonely Saturday morning.

2.

Remembers the round shoulder of water that edged its way
into a rock she used to lie on as a youth in summer, basking inside
a few hours of afternoon light,

then names this place a *bay*.

3.

Forms an *mmmmmm* sound with her lips when her daughter explains,
yet again, what it means to know oneself better
via algorithms and long questionnaires on the internet—

and this youthful voice reminds her of sugar.

4.

Polishes the *sill* holding her plants
before setting one there after watering,
then pauses to stare out through the window's screen mesh
hoping for a token of enchantment.

5.

Lets the scent of daffodils waft *in*
while tasting the chicken still baking in the oven
in her mouth

long before savoring a bite.

THE OPTIMIST IMAGINES WHAT IT WOULD BE LIKE IF HER DAUGHTER WERE ACTUALLY DEAD

Her daughter's breath is deliberate and quiet, a body wombed
against a pillow, fleece blanket wrapped tight over shoulders,
sleeping long into the morning,
then waking with bed-tossed hair on head.

She looks up and smiles to greet her,
having been up for hours with a book about living in the country.
Earth is the great decomposer it says.[1]

She's been thinking about this,
how the mulch outside her window in a shrub bed says something
about dependency; and (not to be morbid)
but how many bodies are feeding those bushy plants?

There's not one of us who isn't in some way eternal. Her daughter
plans to become an animal doctor,
starts talking about rescue operations, holds up a photo of a sweet
little dog who seems to be smiling
having been fed a lit firecracker once.

Her daughter laughs at a video of a young woman playing with a white
tiger pup. The flowers on a cherry tree quiver.

---

[1] *Trauma Farm*, Brian Brett, pg. 81

THE OPTIMIST'S WORLD IS TRANSFORMED
BY ONE PHONE CALL

She stares at the bed her daughter slept in during her visit,
examines the room now tidy, takes stock of the extra things she owns
stored in the guest closet—the way the space seems to suggest
absence. Divorce

feels like a casket missing its body.
Nothing to gather into one's arms for a good long cry.

It's like a war ending,
limbs shattered and left in a foreign country. You can't
go back there.

She hasn't spoken to her son much since the family made its ending.
Now, a pandemic; now
all the questions about what her life has meant.

Even the clothes she wore while married seem a little bloody
with memories she wants to let go of but never forget.

She finds an earring left on top of the bedside table; pearl studded
and golden, tiny, she rolls it between a finger and thumb
as her phone begins to vibrate against the kitchen counter—
she goes out to retrieve it, sees the name pulsing on the screen,
holds it gently.

Answers.

THE OPTIMIST'S SON LEARNS ABOUT LOVE

He talks about her as though she is a plant—something that will grow
with sunshine.

Every day, he says, she asks if he will leave her—sometimes
several times an hour—and every time he answers *No* back.

In a modern age, young love is a sort of disorder,
a bond triggering our more mature fears. She feels herself flinching
against the phone when he speaks of his new love's hair and lips,
her eyes green-gold and shimmery.

At barely twenty, he says he's been waiting for "the one"
and now, he tells her, he's found her;

so she listens and lingers on each pitched syllable—joy, she thinks. Yes,
she remembers this,
a feeling that *today* is magic enough.

They plan an outing for some time in the future (after quarantine)—
a warm afternoon of beaches and sunlight
when she can finally meet her. He's already
writing a menu for the picnic: egg salad and turkey,
white bread, cut carrots, and peanut butter cookies,
a light beer for you Mom, he adds, pausing—*and a bag of granola*
with chocolate for my sister. We should all be together again.

THE OPTIMIST CUTS A NEW PLANT

It feels good to make something new, place a stem in water, watch
it root. Psychologists say we all need someone to care for,
that this is survival: hugging a loved one, playing with a toddler, helping
a neighbor mend a broken fence,

even stopping to consider the plight of a stranger—altruistic, yet not.

Her body depends on the leaves now falling over this glass vase edge
as she lifts a heart-shaped limb with one of her fingers—
handshake perhaps—and smiles, converses,
says *you can do this little plant.*

A nurse, somewhere, has perfected this same motion,
spending another hour by a window fingering its shade with a freshly
gloved hand as she drinks her sixth cup of coffee,
each thin strip of aluminum open to an evening of dark orange
and purple stretched across a sky—

the eyelid of the outside world predictably closing.

THE OPTIMIST DOESN'T TALK ABOUT EVERYTHING

On Facebook she keeps it simple: a meme here, funny video there,
a few updates on her daily life. She made

homemade pizza yesterday—not something
she has done before: turkey bacon, organic tomatoes, and goat cheese
on hand-tossed egg-brushed crust.
It was good
and that's what she said with the picture she posted, a large slice
of pizza posed next to her face.

She recalls the first time she decided to write she was *lonely*
in the Facebook text box,
and that she used too much space.

There are rules for how much you can say when you are hurting—
don't tell a story
as though you are a story;

only say briefly *it's been a rough day.*
To which someone will respond *I hope you feel better* and add a sad face.

In her notebook this evening, she writes sixteen pages
on nothing
then stows it away.

The pizza grows cold in the kitchen till morning. She opens her eyes.
She'd been crying.

THE OPTIMIST DECIDES TO DRAFT A FUTURE PLANT SHOP

She's been working hard at a career for years now to keep herself
from going a little insane.

That's not what she says at work
where she smiles constantly, living off the perks—office chocolate,
luncheons, opportunities for extra pay. She's the woman
that makes a room seem a little brighter,
even the rooms with no windows,
halogen lights, long plastic tables, and other faux things.

She's the woman that makes this look easy, like climbing a ladder
is about floating up.

Her outfits are stylish even when yoga; her hair quite bouncy.

As the world grows more frightened, six feet of distance
between each living body, *stay home!* megaphoned all over
TV commercials and media feeds, no one (she assumes)would imagine
she feels this isolation deeply.

It's a long Sunday.

Grabbing a pad of blank paper, she pencils a sketch of a large room
with tables, chairs, and some books about soil,
sketches a Chemex and selection of teas, puts a name above the door,
writes "Open."

THE OPTIMIST REMEMBERS WHAT IS NEEDED TO FEEL ESSENTIAL

She finds a dollar in a pocket,
feels the thrill of a child. Wonders how long it's been since her hand
explored this space.

The last thing her husband said to her was *no one will want you*
after this. Maybe he was right.

She turns the pocket inside out to see what else it has collected,
finds only lint. She takes this as a metaphor
for value, folding it back into place. She'll have

choices to make when the virus is over; for instance,
this apartment has not been so good for her plants. Things grow
in a balance of sunlight and shade—and their need of each
is different. She drops

green medicine into the water she will give them today, wanting
to believe that the future will be *normal*,
but already, she observes, paranoia has rooted itself into our new forms
of faith. Since

divorce she has also believed the things he told her—words
are chemical in origin, powerful

when mixed.

A spider plant thrives on a shelf in her bedroom, having everything
it needs to sprawl and reproduce.

It's May 22nd.
A gloomy Friday afternoon.

Her daughter will use FaceTime to reach her in an hour;
she'll answer with a smile that brightens the screen—an enormous
and pre-planned *Hello.*

THE OPTIMIST SLEEPS THROUGH THE NIGHT

not because the world has changed
or her life has changed

or the thunderstorm darkening the stars
was suddenly somehow soothing

but because she slept on her stomach and her head burrowed into
the pillow just right.
She predicts she will sleep this way again,
and that the next night will lend itself beautifully to slumber.

The rain softens its pulse by 5AM,
dedicating this morning to whispers. Somewhere
a fever has broken.

Somewhere a young man wakes
to discover the sound of his own breathing—how much like love it is.

An exhale of carbon monoxide
and hope.

He wakes this new morning without a companion,
the plastic around him removed as he slept. The wheels
of his bed suggesting direction,

grey skies outside his window—promising.

NOTES

In "COVID-19 Is Making America's Loneliness Epidemic Even Worse" published by TIME Magazine online on May 8, 2020, Jamie Ducharme highlights the rising number of people living alone and the stigmas associated with expressing one's loneliness publicly. Loneliness, as the article explains, can be as damaging to one's health as smoking 15 cigarettes a day and significantly contribute to "dementia, depression, anxiety, self-harm, heart conditions and substance abuse." It can afflict anyone of any demographic. While making some recommendations about how loneliness can be addressed in daily life, the article mostly draws attention to this "sidelined" issue and the fact that COVID has surfaced our need to address loneliness on a cultural level—stigmatizing less—and becoming more cognizant of everyone's need for social support.

A special thank you to Rosanna Gargiulo, editor of *The Maine Review*, for calling our attention to the "loneliness epidemic" in the United states and including a link to "COVID-19 Is Making America's Loneliness Epidemic Even Worse," in *Maine Review*'s Issue 6.1 *Letter from the Editor*. I had the distinct pleasure of working with this publication's *Embody* feature at the time.

All pandemic statistics in these poems are based on those communicated via news media at the time the poems were written. According to the CDC, there were approximately 375,000 COVID-related deaths in the United States alone by the end of 2020, becoming the third leading cause of death in the US during that year.

Anne Stevenson, poet, Sylvia Plath biographer, and author of "In the House," died at age 87 of heart failure in her home in England on September 14, 2020 as the pandemic raged around the globe.

Finally, thank you to my beautiful, talented, and beloved daughter, Ryley Eden Priest, for visiting with me during the pandemic in person and over FaceTime. You are my best friend, the joy of my life, and the reason I keep breathing through every difficult moment. I love you.

ACKNOWLEDGMENT

The Laurel Review: "The Optimist Continues to Consider the Weather"

Kimberly Ann Priest is the author of *Slaughter the One Bird* (Sundress 2021), finalist for the American Best Book Award, as well as the chapbooks *Parrot Flower* (Glass 2021), *Still Life* (PANK 2020), and *White Goat Black Sheep* (Finishing Line Press 2018). Winner of the *New American Press* 2019 Heartland Poetry Prize, her work has appeared in journals such as *North Dakota Quarterly, Salamander, Slipstream, The Berkeley Poetry Review, EcoTheo, Borderlands* and many others. She is an associate poetry editor for the *Nimrod International Journal of Prose and Poetry* and assistant professor at Michigan State University. Find her work at kimberlyannpriest.com.

Made in the USA
Middletown, DE
13 August 2023

36644107R00026